BASS LEGENDARY LICKS
METALLICA

Other Metallica Legendary Licks books available:

Metallica Legendary Licks Guitar 1983-1988 02500181
Metallica Legendary Licks Guitar 1988-1996 02500182
Metallica Legendary Licks Drums 02500172

Recording Credits:
Tom McGir, bass
Doug Boduch, guitar
Scott Schroedl, drums
Jake Johnson, recording and mixing engineer
Todd Greene, producer

Cover photography by Ross Halfin/Idols

ISBN 1-57560-288-1

Visit our website at www.cherrylane.com

Introduction

The early 1980s: glam-rock predominated the loosely defined heavy metal genre. Rock groups with teased hair and make-up pumped out sugarcoated pop songs that filled the airwaves. It was in this unlikely state of affairs that a four-man aural assault called Metallica emerged from the San Francisco Bay Area and tore its way into music history. The group's conquest began in 1983 when their debut album, *Kill 'Em All,* sent a jolt into the ears of metal fans and critics alike and has continued, with ever-growing successes, to the present day.

As Metallica continues to break new ground and compound its own legend, there are no limits in sight. And now, with this book, there is no limit to what you can learn about how the bass guitar has contributed to that success.

Metallica Bass Legendary Licks presents a comprehensive play-along package that includes note-for-note transcriptions and recordings. The transcriptions present every note, in tablature and standard notation, just as Cliff Burton and Jason Newsted played them. There are no vocals on the CD, so it's easy to hear exactly what the instruments are doing. You'll also find slowed-down versions of the fast and tricky passages, which make the learning process that much simpler. The detailed performance notes in the book will give you insightful perspectives on your favorite Metallica songs and help you play them even better. Further, the recording is *split channel,* so you can listen to all the instruments *or* play along with the band. In short, listen and learn—and you'll be thrashing and shredding in no time.

Photo by Ross Halfin/Idols

Photo by Anton Corbijn

Contents

Editor's Note: Tune bass down a whole step (D G C F) for "Sad but True" and down a half step (E♭ A♭ D♭ G♭) for all songs on *Load* and *Reload*.

A Historical Retrospective of Metallica

Kill 'Em All (1983)

Early Metallica music is known for the abrasive, in-your-face production and songwriting. *Kill 'Em All*—the song "Seek & Destroy," in particular—is a perfect example. Cliff Burton used a Rickenbacker bass, wah pedal, distortion pedal, and Marshall guitar amplifiers on this recording; the cumulative result is a tone that is full of growl and reminiscent of Motorhead's Lemmy Kilmister. Most of Burton's bass lines are based closely on the songs' riffs, which is characteristic of thrash and speed metal bass parts and tends to create a thick, heavy texture. Burton's use of lead guitar techniques, combined with his tremendous chops and complementary ensemble playing, added greatly to the album's ferociousness and set a new standard for heavy metal bass.

Ride the Lightning (1984)

With *Ride the Lightning*, Metallica's music, as well as the subject matter of their lyrics, had reached a new level of maturity. Exploring topics as varied as capital punishment and an Ernest Hemingway novel, *Ride the Lightning*—the world's first taste of heavy metal with a conscience—brought Metallica praise from influential music critics and broader recognition worldwide. It was an early example of Metallica's remarkable ability to strive for new horizons with every album rather than rely on a formula. This unrelenting drive has played a huge role in their continued success over the years.

Master of Puppets (1985)

On *Master of Puppets*, which many consider the ultimate metal album, Metallica displayed both a charged vitality and a confrontational edge. While still advancing artistically, they managed to retain the youthful honesty that had made the earlier albums so successful. *Master of Puppets* was a breakthrough for Metallica and heavy metal itself, for metal had never seen such elaborate musical ideas—nor such weighty subject matter, such as drug addiction and war.

. . . And Justice for All (1988)

It is probably not accidental that green and black were chosen for *. . . And Justice for All's* cover art, for its title track deals with the evils (black) of money (green) while "Blackened" speaks of the end (black) of the earth (green). *. . . And Justice For All* marked a first and a last for Metallica: it was the first album with Jason Newsted on bass (following Cliff Burton's tragic death) and the last of Metallica's collaborations with long-time producer Flemming Rasmussen. Newsted's bass tone is generally cleaner than that of his predecessor, mostly because he played Wal and ESP custom basses instead of Burton's more primitive gear. This unique album will be remembered as Metallica's most extreme venture into the world of musical complexity.

Metallica (1991)

Perhaps in direct response to the slightly esoteric musical complexity of *. . . And Justice For All, Metallica* was the group's most accessible album to date and caught the ears of many new listeners who had never enjoyed Metallica's music before. Its more traditional arrangements and "radio-friendly" production still captured the aggression that had earned Metallica its headbanging loyalists, but was now better suited for MTV and other mass outlets. Surely the biggest catalyst in these changes was the designation of Bob Rock as producer for the album. Rock had a distinct influence on many aspects of Metallica's sound, from production methods to stylistic choices.

Load (1996)

Load clearly demonstrated that the group had continued to grow musically in the five years since *Metallica*. One of the album's many assets was bringing the musical voices of Kirk Hammet and, in particular, Jason Newsted to the foreground. A second was the group's decision to, for the first time, record the drum and bass tracks prior to the other tracks, which would establish a tight rhythmic foundation upon which the remaining instruments could build. Though *Metallica* had planted the seeds for change in the group's style, it was *Load* and the subsequent *Reload* that brought about a feeling of unlimited new potential among the members of Metallica.

Reload (1997)

Reload was essentially a continuation of *Load*, as all of the songs were written during the same period of great inspiration that led up to *Load*. Deadlines for the completion of *Load's* recording, coupled with the abundance of worthy material, led to a decision in January 1996 to divide the songs into two equally strong batches and release the second as a separate follow-up album in 1997.

Where will Metallica go next? Regardless of the answer, one can trust that the essential qualities that have been the hallmarks of their remarkable success—honest delivery, rigorous self-improvement, and the drive for artistic innovation, to name just a few—will continue to thrill their millions of devoted fans.

About the Author

James A. Rota II is an all-around musician's musician. He received a bachelor's degree from The College Conservatory of Music at the University of Cincinnati. Rota is also a recording/touring artist with the band Fireball Ministry, on Bong Load Records. Rota lives and breathes in Los Angeles, CA.

James A. Rota II

Visit the Rev. James A. Rota II and his church at www.fireballministry.com

The Metallica Workout

To play some of Metallica's flashiest licks and riffs, you need to have superhuman finger dexterity. Sure you could acquire these herculean chops by spending your days locked away in a practice room, with a bass guitar and a metronome, doing 12-hour marathon practice sessions of scales, arpeggios, and exercises . . . but there's a better way.

Some of Metallica's legendary licks and riffs also make great finger exercises that can be used both as a warm-up before playing and as part of a daily practice regimen. The benefits of this approach are twofold: you have an effective technique-building routine that allows you to accurately gauge your progress and you end up learning some cool riffs and licks in the process.

Here's the practice strategy. Start each practice session always playing the exercise at the same tempo marking (you'll need a metronome for this). Move the metronome up one notch at a time, but only when you feel absolutely confident that you are playing the exercise accurately and cleanly. When you've reached the last metronome marking at which you can play the exercise cleanly, mark the number down and make it your goal to match this tempo—and even beat it—in the next practice session.

Here are some things to think about as you practice these exercises.

Left Hand

- Are your fingers pressing the fretboard properly and producing a good sound?
- Are your fingers coming too far off the fretboard as you change notes?

Right Hand

- Are you using too much right-hand pressure? Too little?
- If you are using alternate fingers, are you sure your strokes are in fact alternating?

Timing/Rhythm

- Are all the notes evenly spaced? Are you rushing or dragging?

The Metallica Workout *Cont.*

Exercise 1

The "Master of Puppets" intro riff makes for a great exercise, as it incorporates all four left-hand fingers.

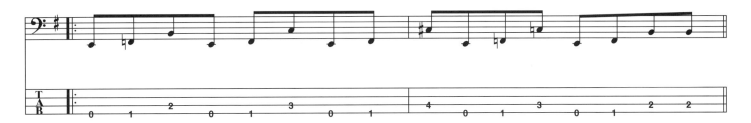

Exercise 2

This is the "Damage, Inc." bass line heard under the guitar solo. Concentrate on evenness and accuracy in your right hand.

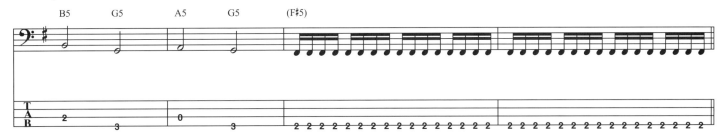

Exercise 3

Here is the "Seek and Destroy" blues scale lick. This is another four-finger, left-hand exercise, but this time with shifting positions.

Tone Clone: How to Replicate the Metallica Bass Sound

Cliff Burton's Tone

To achieve a bass tone similar to Cliff Burton's you will need some essential tools. First, a bass that has a naturally defined mid-range and thick low-end, such as a Rickenbacker 4001 or a Fender Precision Bass. If your bass does not have inherently prominent mids and lows, you can raise these frequencies on your amp using the tone controls or use an EQ pedal to boost these frequencies.

Next, an amp with one or two 15-inch speakers is perfect for bringing out the lower frequencies. Using 15-inch speakers in combination with a bottom-heavy bass, you might find that the tone can become muddy and indistinguishable. This leads us to the next step.

The lack of high-end in this rig will be aided by the addition of a fuzz pedal. A fuzz pedal will allow low bass notes to cut through. Choose a pedal that allows you to adjust the level of gain (sometimes called *drive*) so that you can find a comfort zone where the bass won't feedback or sound over-saturated yet will still have some bite.

Jason Newsted's Tone

Jason Newsted's tone is considerably brighter and cleaner than Cliff Burton's. Aside from Newsted's use of the pick as the preferred right-hand method, a more contemporary approach is taken equipment-wise (not to mention a lot more money spent!) towards achieving tonal nirvana.

Newsted's basses, usually Sadowskys, are custom made. These instruments, while having a higher price tag, also have a distinguished tone with a wider range frequency range with plenty of highs. If your bass does not naturally have these characteristics, you can raise the treble either on your amp on an EQ pedal to achieve the desired brightness. As you do so, be sure to retain enough mids and lows in your sound to maintain thickness.

Some of Newsted's bass lines feature notes played on a five-string bass tuned to low B. If you don't have a five-string bass, try using the bottom four strings from a five-string set on your bass.

Finally, a speaker cabinet with 10-inch speakers will provide the clarity and definition characteristic of Newsted's bass sound. You should use an amp that has a cleaner front end (i.e. with a clean-sounding preamp section). Just remember that his tone relies on a clean sounding instrument and amplifier. No mud here—just clean-and-fat power.

Gear Setup

Cliff Burton

Cliff Burton's live setup included an Aria Pro II bass and a Rickenbacker bass played through a Mesa Boogie amp with a Mesa Boogie 2 x 15 cabinet. His effects included an Electro-Harmonix Big Muff and a Morley Power Wah Boost pedal.

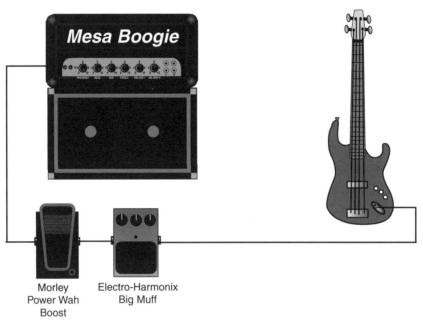

Morley
Power Wah
Boost

Electro-Harmonix
Big Muff

Jason Newsted

Jason Newsted generally plays a Sadowsky basses through an Ampeg SVT amp with an Ampeg 8 x 10 cabinet. His effects include a Boss flanger, MXR phase 100, Korg G5 bass synth processor, Electro-Harmonix Big Muff, and a Morley Power Wah Boost.

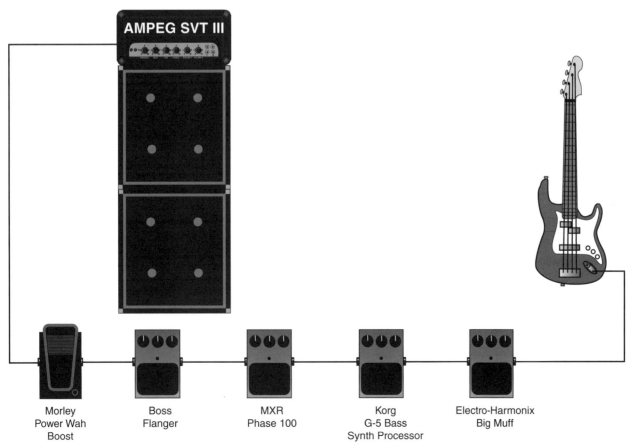

Morley
Power Wah
Boost

Boss
Flanger

MXR
Phase 100

Korg
G-5 Bass
Synth Processor

Electro-Harmonix
Big Muff

• BASS TABLATURE EXPLANATION/NOTATION LEGEND •

Bass tablature is a four-line staff that graphically represents the bass fingerboard. By placing a number on the appropriate line, the string and fret of any note can be indicated. The number 0 represents an open string. For example:

1st string - G
2nd string - D
3rd string - A
4th string - E

3rd string, 3rd fret   4th string, open

_____ Definitions for Special Bass Notation (for both traditional and tablature bass lines) _____

BEND: Strike the note and bend up 1/2 step (one fret).

BEND: Strike the note and bend up whole step (two frets).

BEND AND RELEASE: Strike the note. Bend up 1/2 (or whole) step, then release the bend back to the original note. All three notes are tied; only the first note is struck.

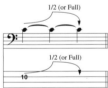

PRE-BEND: Bend the note up 1/2 (or whole) step, then strike it.

PRE-BAND AND RELEASE: Bend the note up 1/2 (or whole) step. Strike it and release the bend back to the original note.

VIBRATO: Vibrate the note by rapidly bending and releasing it with the left hand.

SLIDE: Strike the first note and then with the same left-hand finger move up the string to the location of the second note. The second note is not struck.

SLIDE: Same as above except the second note is struck.

SLIDE: Slide up to the note indicated from a few frets below.

SLIDE: Strike the note and slide up an indefinite number of frets, releasing finger pressure at the end of the slide.

HAMMER ON: Strike the first (lower) note, then sound the higher note with another finger by fretting it without picking.

PULL-OFF: Place both fingers on the notes to be sounded. Strike the first (higher) note, then sound the lower note by pulling the finger off the higher note while keeping the lower note fretted.

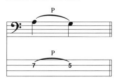

TAPPING: Hammer ("tap") the fret indicated with the right-hand index or middle finger and pull off to the note fretted by the left hand ("T" indicates "tapped" notes).

NATURAL HARMONIC: With a left-hand finger, lightly touch the string over the fret indicated, then strike it. A chime-like sound is produced.

ARTIFICIAL HARMONIC: Fret the note normally and sound the harmonic by lightly touching the node point on the string with the edge of the right hand thumb while simultaneously plucking with the right-hand index or middle finger.

PALM MUTE: If using a pick, partially mute the note by lightly touching the string with the right hand just before the bridge.

SLAP AND POP: Slap (•) the string with the side of the thumb. Pop (ↄ), or snap, the styring wth the index or middle finger by pulling and releasing it so that it rebounds against the fretboard.

MUFFLED STRINGS: Lay the left hand across the string without depressing it to the fretboard. Strike the string with the right hand, producing a percussive sound.

Seek & Destroy

from *Kill 'Em All*

Words and Music by
James Hetfield and Lars Ulrich
Copyright © 1983 Creeping Death Music (ASCAP)
International Copyright Secured All Rights Reserved

"There is no escape and that is for sure, this is the end we won't take anymore. Say goodbye to the world you live in, you have always been taking but now you're giving."

Were these thoughts directed at the L.A. scene? Soon after this song, Metallica left town and relocated to San Francisco upon bassist Cliff Burton's beckoning.

Intro

The bass part in the introduction of this song is characterized by a prevalence of accents. After playing A almost exclusively for 10 bars, Burton grooves with the drums in a riff centered on E until bar 26. At that point the song's basic groove is established, and Burton's eighth-note figure, though still full of accents, becomes much steadier rhythmically. He marks the end of every second bar with a two-beat fill based on the E blues scale (E G A B B♭ D), which emphasizes the tritone, or flatted 5th.

TRACK 01

Full Band

TRACK 02

Slow Demo

Moderate Rock ♩ = 140

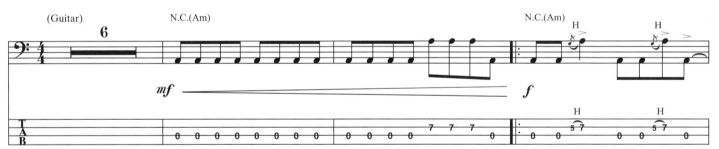

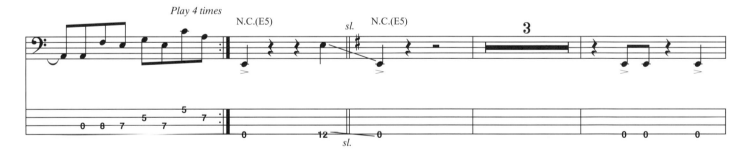

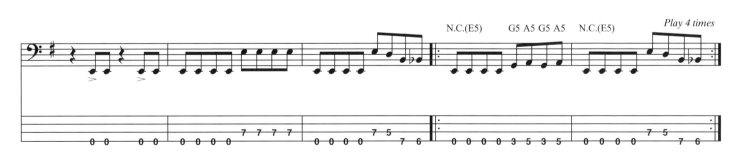

Pre-Chorus

A pre-chorus, as the name implies, sets up the chorus, giving you the sense that something is coming. It is typically found between the verse and the chorus, and is commonly based on a different tonal center than these sections.

This pre-chorus is a prime example: it is based on A pentatonic minor (A C D E G), in contrast to the verse and chorus, both of which are based primarily on E pentatonic minor (E G A B D). Burton's bass part breaks away from the constant eighth-note activity of these sections by introducing quarter notes, which effectively add rhythmic tension. Also notice how the unison E blues scale lick at the end of the phrase leads right into the chorus.

TRACK 03

Full Band

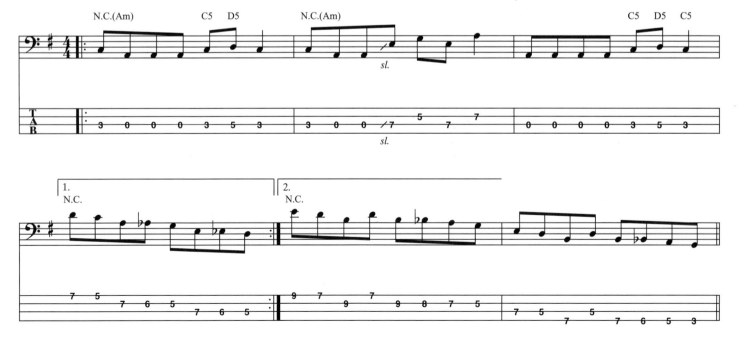

Solo

In the pre-chorus, Metallica marked off sections by changing the harmony; for this guitar solo, they do so simply by increasing the tempo. The bass descends chromatically, from G to E, over the first two bars and then settles into an eighth-note feel with many octave leaps. The solo ends with the whole band playing a descending eighth-note riff into an A harmony with a *fermata* (a hold). This train-wreck style ending has been used for centuries as a way to conclude a phrase or section—listen to a Haydn symphony for proof!

TRACK 04

Full Band

For Whom the Bell Tolls

from *Ride the Lightning*

Words and Music by
James Hetfield, Lars Ulrich and Cliff Burton

Which came first: the chicken or the egg? In rock music, the equivalent of that question might deal with the music and the lyrics. The subject matter of "For Whom the Bell Tolls," based the Ernest Hemingway novel of the same name, is about the Spanish Civil War, and its march-like groove seems to imply that the lyrics preceded the music. The song has an effective militaristic feel from the opening bells to the dramatic finish.

Introduction

After the two triplet hits in the opening, Burton plays a scorching riff that listeners often mistake for guitar. It is a combination of his use of wah and distortion, and his playing uncharacteristically high-register notes that alters the tone in this passage. After 16 bars of the intro riff, Burton switches to the eighth-note pattern that will be the main pulse of the song, and the rest of the band follows suit in bar 27. Metallica's unison playing is offset by drum accents on the upbeats of beat 1. In the next section, the rhythm section establishes a straightforward march groove, with Burton pounding out quarter notes and eighth-note triplets, while the lead guitar plays an ominous triplet ostinato. Finally, the group plays unison quarter-note triplets that lead into the first verse.

TRACK 05 — Full Band   **TRACK 06** — Slow Demo (Bass II)

Fade to Black

from *Ride the Lightning*

Words and Music by
James Hetfield, Lars Ulrich, Cliff Burton and Kirk Hammett

"Fade to Black"—with its minor key, slow tempo, and arpeggiated guitar chords—is a true metal ballad. It is surprising to find this song on the same album as "Fight Fire with Fire" and "Trapped Under Ice," as it is the only song on the album that speaks of resignation, and the only one not to fight death but accept it. It also features some of the most dramatic playing Cliff Burton ever recorded.

Introduction

The song's opening synthesized crescendo (not on CD) sets up the first intro riff, a four-bar pattern that arpeggiates the chord progression. In the first 20 bars of the song, the bass is used to accent the drum hits at the beginning of each riff. The figured bass pattern of bars 21–23 serves as a springboard into the main section of the song.

TRACK 07

Full Band

Interlude

This section consists of a four-bar riff played four times, creating two eight-bar phrases. The bass's pattern is the same in every pass except for some variations in the fourth bar of each. The powerful material in this passage, coupled with Metallica's tight unison playing, effectively captures the aggression that can grow out of despair.

TRACK 08
Full Band

TRACK 09
Slow Demo

Battery

from *Master of Puppets*

Words and Music by
James Hetfield and Lars Ulrich

Don't be fooled by the tranquil acoustic guitar opening: "Battery" is one brutal trasher that will "crush all deceivers" and "mash non-believers."

Introduction

After the solo acoustic section, Burton reinforces the rhythmic hits that build up to the frenzied main riff of the song. At first, play bars 30–40 slowly with a metronome. As you get more comfortable with these bars, work your way up to the actual tempo. This is the first example of actual thrash metal that we have encountered. . . .

TRACK 10

Full Band

Battery *Cont.*

Guitar Solo

During the guitar solo, James Hetfield plays a modified version of the original eight-bar riff. Burton, with careful rhythmic precision, plays a driving sixteenth- and eighth-note phrase under the riff. The riff is played twice and followed by an extended version of the tag that was first played at the end of the introduction. The original three bars of the tag moved harmonically in a rising motion; in this extended version, an extra bar has been added with the chord in the added fourth bar leading back down by step to the first chord. The fifth and sixth bars are the same as the first and second. The seventh bar begins like the third but is interrupted by a two-bar, double bass drum break that rounds off the eight-bar musical idea. Also notice, in the majority of this section, how Burton plays two sixteenth notes on the second half of beat 3 to create extra momentum leading up to the break.

TRACK 11 — Full Band

TRACK 12 — Slow Demo

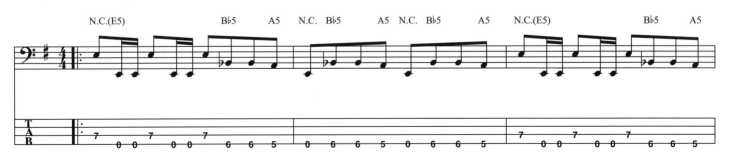

Master of Puppets

from **Master of Puppets**

Words and Music by
James Hetfield, Lars Ulrich, Kirk Hammett and Cliff Burton

It is not obvious at first glance how to relate the lyrics of this song with the cover art of the album. The words are about the destruction of life due to drugs, while the army helmet and dogtag around two crosses on the cover might suggest that the "master" is the government or the military. Perhaps Metallica was referring to the widespread rumor about the U.S. military supplying American soldiers in Vietnam with various drugs while on duty. . . .

Introduction

This introduction is comprised of opening unison chord jabs that lead into three main riffs. The first riff, a chromatically descending line (from E down to F♯) wedged between a low, open-E pedal, is an expansion of the chromatically descending chord gesture heard in the opening (D, D♭, and C). The bass lays out here, only entering to give a downbeat in the first bar and catching the quarter-note, chromatic descent in the second bar. This paves the way for the second riff, a four-bar chromatic line that first ascends and then descends (from B to C♯) against a pedal of low E's and F's, finishing each phrase with sliding power chord punctuations. This riff is played twice and followed by an eight-bar extended and slightly altered (the sliding power chords are replaced with a quarter-note chord in the fourth bar) version of it, with the bass joining in unison. After a total of six repetitions, the third riff enters. This riff, a four-bar phrase with an unexpected meter change to $\frac{6}{8}$ in the fourth bar, is simply a low, open-E pedal (this time without any chromatic interjections) that alternates with the sliding power chord idea taken from the second riff.

TRACK 13
Full Band

TRACK 14
Slow Demo

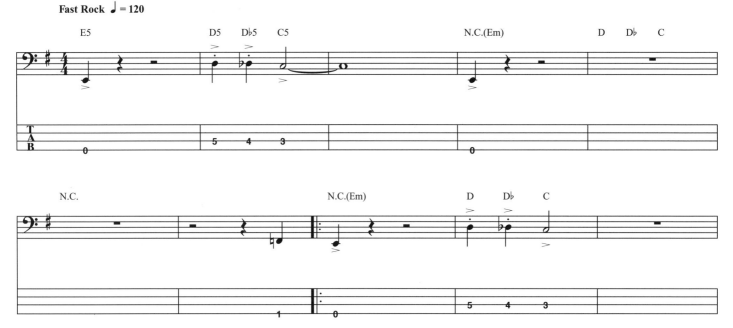

Pre-Chorus

A four-bar riff is repeated here four times and followed by the infamous "master . . . master . . ." chant. When the rhythm switches to a half time feel, the syncopated drum groove can lead to some confusion. In order to feel the groove, pay attention to how the bass part fits with both the guitar line and the placement of the drum accents. It is also advised that you listen to the section a few times without looking at the music before you attempt to play it, that way you will be sure to capture the feel, which might remain elusive if you only look at the printed page.

TRACK 15

Full Band

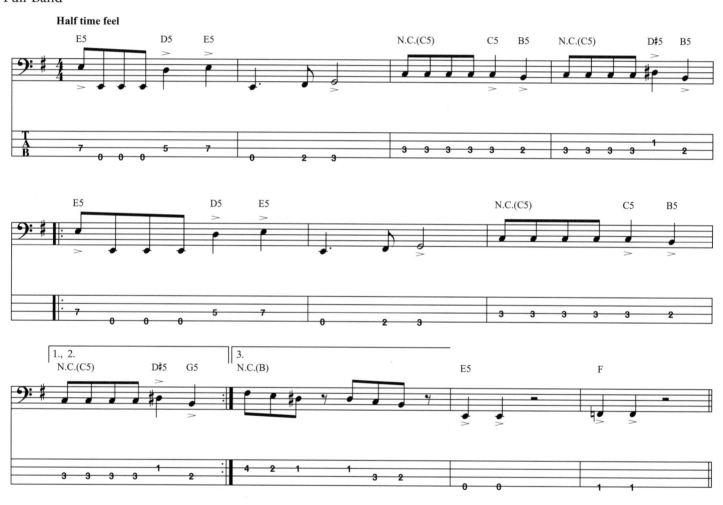

Interlude

The guitar begins this section with an arpeggiated four-bar riff whose sudden tranquillity provides an effective contrast to the prior material. During the second and third passes, the riff is harmonized by the bass and a second guitar. As in "Fade to Black," the bass part here functions similarly to the left hand of a piano player. In bar 9, the drums switch to a straightforward rock groove, and the bass adjusts accordingly to a more rhythmic feel.

TRACK 16

Full Band

Slower ♩ = 110

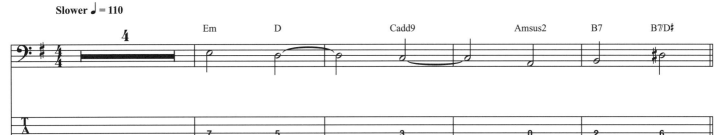

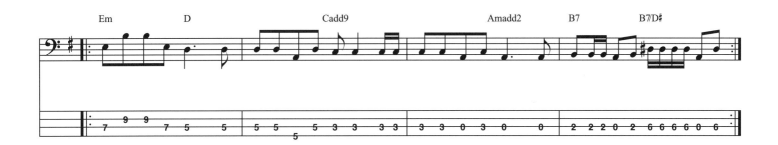

Welcome Home (Sanitarium)

from *Master of Puppets*

Words and Music by
James Hetfield, Lars Ulrich and Kirk Hammett

The title "Welcome Home" addresses a soldier returning from war. The song is thus a continuation of the military theme from "Master of Puppets," which Metallica also takes up in "Disposable Heroes."

Introduction

Several bars of mellow, E minor-based material set up the introduction's three-bar main riff. The riff, with its uncommon ten-beat rhythmic construction, outlines the inner-voice harmonic movement of the guitar and introduces passing tones and neighbor tones in the last repetition before the vocals enter.

TRACK 17

Full Band

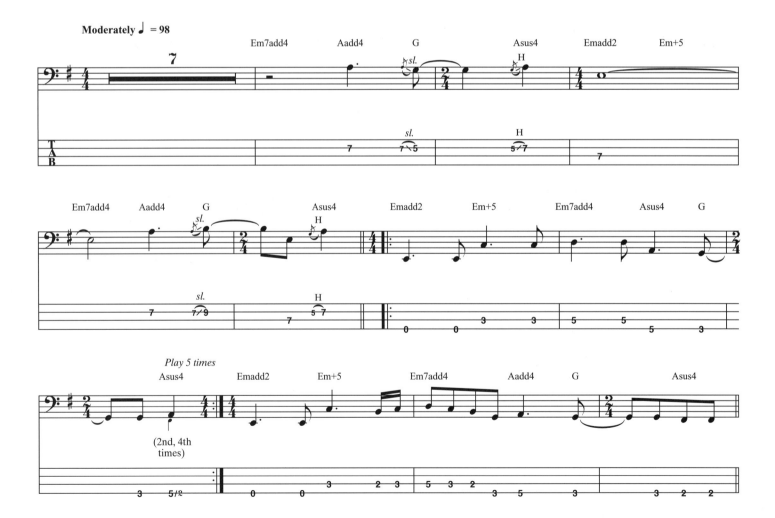

Chorus

The mood of the guitar riff here is in sharp contrast to that of the verse. The overall energy picks up considerably (as does the tempo, though perhaps accidentally!), while the rhythm becomes much more dense. This rigorous section will surely feel like a workout for you. First, there are the choked sixteenth notes, which can be produced by muting the strings with the left hand and picking with the right at normal velocity. Then, there are the sixteenth-note runs, which you most likely will need to play slowly at first, and finally the tricky sixteenth-note triplet that rounds out the first and third phrase, which requires accurately timed hammer-ons and pull-offs. Whew! If you take a break to rest your chops, listen to the group's impressive unison playing in this section.

TRACK 18
Full Band

TRACK 19
Slow Demo

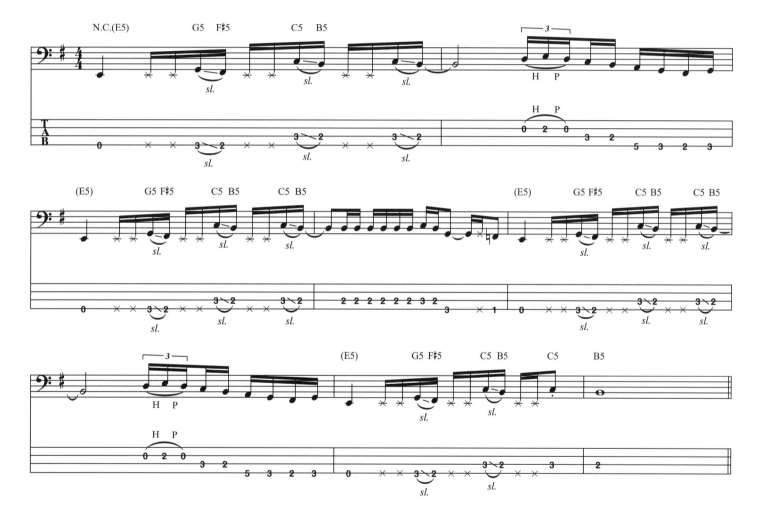

Bridge

This bridge serves as a moment of repose between two double time sections. The rhythmic motive of the guitar riff derives from the double time lick that immediately preceded it. The drum figures and the highly syncopated vocal line, in turn, are connected to the rhythmic structure of the guitar riff, which is also mimicked by the bass.

TRACK 20

Full Band

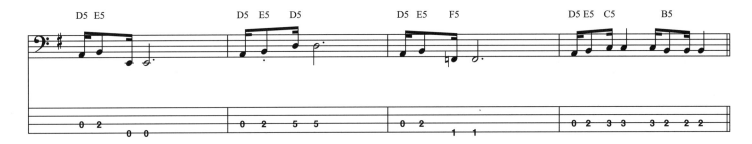

Guitar Solo

This section immediately follows the bridge. At first, the drum part supports the rhythm guitar riff quite closely, but it gradually becomes more independent. Therefore, in order to maintain your rhythmic precision when playing along, pay more attention to the guitar than to the drums or you may get thrown off.

TRACK 21

Full Band

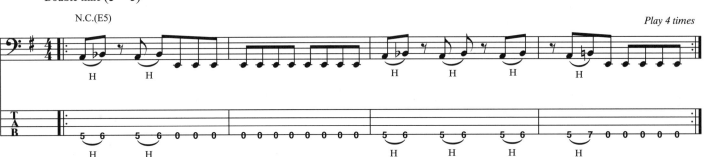

Leper Messiah

from *Master of Puppets*

Words and Music by
James Hetfield and Lars Ulrich

Are they really talking about leprosy? Or rather, about a "disease" that plagues evangelism in America today? The victim of Metallica's lyrics seems to have switched here from the military to Christianity. No one could accuse them of shying away from big targets!

Introduction

This introduction establishes the mood and motivic substance for the rest of the song. After the pickup bar, the band plays eight bars of a unison rhythmic idea—the most important rhythmic idea of the song, in fact, because most of the subsequent riffs derive from it. Be sure to count when playing the long, held notes that give these opening bars their tightness and suspense. The section following the $\frac{3}{4}$ bar is comprised of a four-bar guitar riff played twice. Notice how the ♪♫ ♩ idea of the opening theme is implicit in the bass part. After the riff, the guitar sustains a single chord for four bars and then introduces a two-bar idea that has eighth notes on beats 2 and 4 of the first bar, and beat 2 of the second bar with the bass playing an E natural minor (E F♯ G A B C D) groove throughout. In the fourth pass through the lick, the rhythmic idea from the beginning is tacked onto the end of the first bar. Rather than squeeze the two motives into a $\frac{4}{4}$ bar, Metallica allows this juxtaposition of ideas to result in a unique $\frac{5}{4}$ bar.

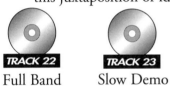

TRACK 22   **TRACK 23**

Full Band   Slow Demo

Medium Rock ♩ = 136

Leper Messiah *Cont.*

Damage, Inc.

from *Master of Puppets*

Words and Music by
James Hetfield, Lars Ulrich, Kirk Hammett and Cliff Burton

There is both an edge and an honesty to the style of this album, and of this song, in particular. Undoubtedly, *Master of Puppets* was the album that showed the world who Metallica was and what they could do. The liner notes from *Ride the Lightning* mention a quest for world domination . . . Metallica was rapidly fulfilling this very destiny.

Introduction

This is a notey bass part, and to keep it steady it would probably be helpful to group the notes into larger units; that is, think of four sixteenth notes as a one-beat unit rather than as four separate entities. The eight-bar sequence is played twice, the second repetition adding a whole-note march idea that leads to a bar of unison sixteenth notes and a surprising $\frac{7}{8}$ bar of silence that sets up the third riff. Making the rest bar $\frac{7}{8}$ was surely intended to throw the listener slightly off-balance as the next groove begins. The final riff, the one-bar verse riff, outlines an E diminished triad (E G B♭) played eight times before a *grand pause* $\frac{2}{4}$ bar sets up the actual verse. Don't over work your wrist practicing this section—take a break if it hurts.

TRACK 24

Full Band

TRACK 25

Slow Demo

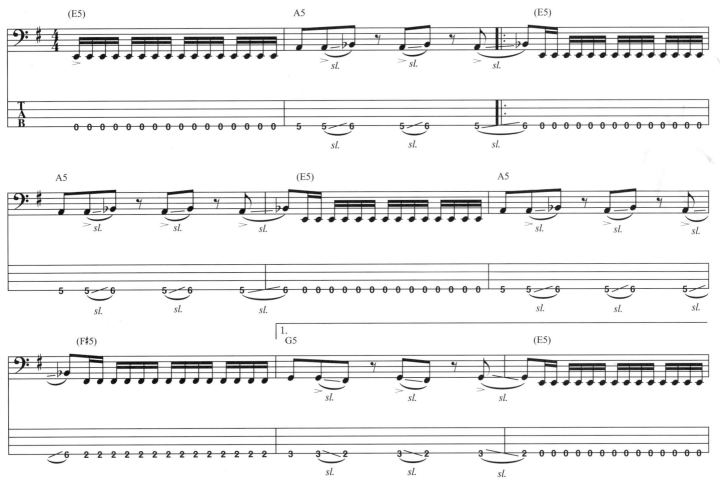

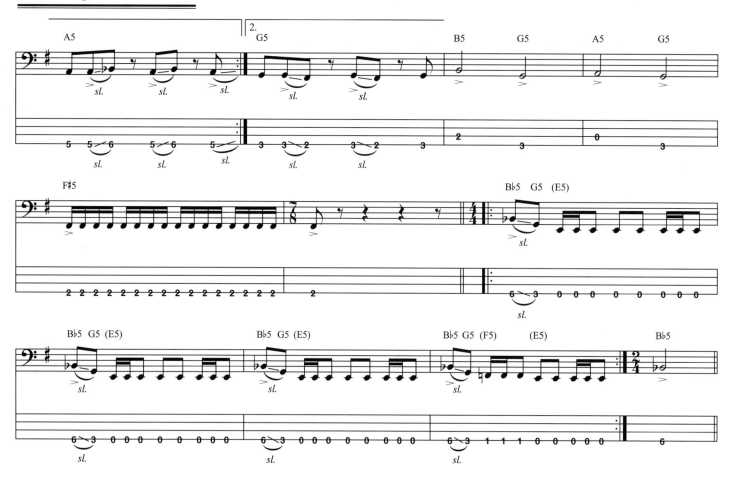

Guitar Solo

The first 16 bars of this section are a fairly static backdrop for the solo: the guitar and bass play a continuous sixteenth-note groove, while the harmony changes just once in the entire 16 bars. The key to making this section work is to focus on evenness and accuracy . . . and to not lose the tempo. The next 16 bars derive primarily from the introductory material with Metallica playing in rhythmic unison at the end.

TRACK 26

Full Band

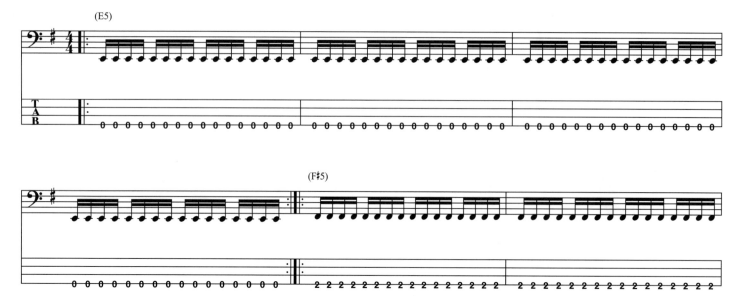

Blackened

from . . . *And Justice for All*

Words and Music by
James Hetfield, Lars Ulrich and Jason Newsted

Blackened contains some of the most intense rhythmical playing that Metallica has ever recorded. Metallica truly manage to throw "all you see into obscurity."

Introduction

Whoa! This is confusing! The first band unison is written out as a 5/4 bar followed by a 7/4 bar where Hetfield begins the Intro Riff. But if you imagine that the figure began on the upbeat eighth note just before the bar, it is possible to hear the rhythmic figure as ♪| ♫ ♩♫ ♫♪ 𝄾𝄾♪ ♪. Viewed from this perspective it bears a resemblance to the rhythmic break motive, ♩♫ ♫ ♫ 𝄽, that is heard throughout the song. The 7/4 riff that follows has a galloping melody centered around the pitch E and based on the E Phrygian mode (E F G A B C D); the riff is stated over an E pedal that fills in the riff's rhythmic gaps. What is fascinating about this riff is the ambiguity of its pulse: either of the two voices in the riff—the melody or the pedal— can be heard as the anchor of time marking the main pulse of the 7/4 bar (beats 1, 3, and 5). Choosing to hear the E pedal as the pulse means that Lars Ulrich is beating upbeat eighth notes on the snare and hi-hat. If he is indeed playing upbeats, it is necessary to conceive the bar before the rhythmic break motive as being in 7/8. However, choosing to hear the primary melodic line as the pulse means that Ulrich is instead beating downbeat quarter notes and, after three 7/4 bars, sliding smoothly into 4/4 for the rhythmic break motive where the bass enters, playing the main riff in unison with the guitar.

So which interpretation is correct? The question is abstract, and the answer is that they both are. A more interesting question is, "How and why did Metallica create this ambiguous passage?!" They must have found this rhythmic ambiguity fascinating, for it had to take a considerable effort on their part to establish it. The passage is followed by two rhythmic break bars and a return of the 7/4 riff for eight more bars—this time, the low E is most decidedly heard as the downbeat. At the end, a riff in 6/4 is played four times in unison with the guitar and bass.

TRACK 27
Full Band

TRACK 28
Slow Demo

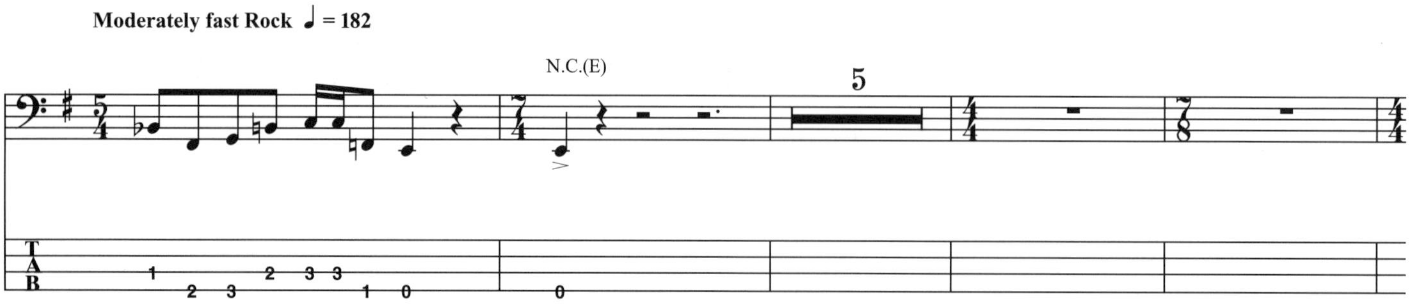
Moderately fast Rock ♩ = 182
N.C.(E)
5
T
A
B
1
2 3
2 3 3
1 0
0

Chorus Riff

Newsted reinforces the chorus by playing chord roots in rhythmic unison with the guitar and providing rhythmic activity in bars 3 and 6, when the guitars and voice are static.

TRACK 29
Full Band

Interlude

Ulrich uses steady quarter notes on the bass drum to establish a new, slower tempo for this section. The guitar enters on beat 4 as a pickup to the four-bar phrase, with the bass holding down a low E until the second repetition of the phrase. Here Newsted begins a steady eighth-note bass line that alternates between a tritone lick and repetitions of the note E.

One

from . . . *And Justice for All*

Words and Music by
James Hetfield and Lars Ulrich

This song became Metallica's first music video. "One" picks up on the themes dealt with in "Master of Puppets" by dramatizing a soldier's disturbing, post-war reality. It is inspired by the book "Johnny Got His Gun" by Dalton Trumbo, in which a young man injured in combat is left with no arms, no legs, *and* no voice. Compare the military ideas here with those of "Disposable Heroes" or "Welcome Home (Sanitarium)." Also, a spiritual theme, which will be developed in "To Live is to Die," is introduced in this song by the soldier's pleas to God.

Introduction

James Hetfield shouts military orders during the battlefield sound effect at the beginning of the song (not on CD). He then plays the eight-bar, arpeggiated guitar riff (in B minor) that is the source for much subsequent material. The first of its three passes is unaccompanied, and the second has an additional guitar track. The bass enters with offbeat, staccato eighth notes in the last bar of the third pass, which has been transformed to a $\frac{4}{4}$ bar instead of $\frac{2}{4}$. After the third pass, the riff continues but is changed to $\frac{3}{4}$ time. In the last eight bars of the section, a four-bar descending harmonic progression is played twice. The bass part in this introduction adds movement to the section (via chord tones and neighbor tones) without ever sounding too busy. Notice the gradual change in rhythmic intensity, with the anchoring dotted quarter-note figure organically evolving into a steady stream of eighths as D, the relative major key, is reached.

TRACK 31

Full Band

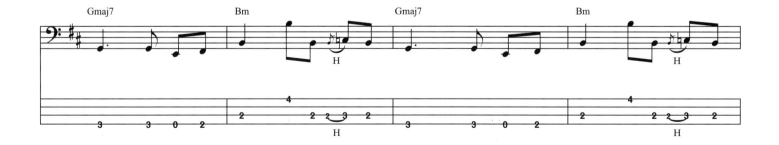

Interlude

After the $\frac{6}{4}$ "Now the world is gone . . ." section, a four-bar chord progression repeats six times. Though the progression is written in $\frac{3}{4}$ time, the drums continue the $\frac{6}{4}$ groove from the previous section, phrasing over the bar lines. After the fourth pass, the first two chords of the phrase are changed, but the ominous B5–C5 cadence remains. Newsted's bass part outlines the chords while adding some non-chord tones (such as the D against the A minor chord and the F against the C chord) to create dissonances that are not immediately resolved. These dissonances add to the sense of despair and sets up the next bombastic section.

TRACK 32

Full Band

Sixteenth-Note Triplet Riff

For the first two bars of this section, Newsted simply plays the trademark sixteenth-note triplet riff on E. In the next three bars, he introduces quarter notes on the second beat (instead of eighths) and a half-step, upward movement (as the last eighth note of the bar) that implies E Phrygian. During the rest of the section, other small variations, like octave displacements, appear sporadically. When Hetfield's vocal begins, he keeps a similar rhythm to the guitar and bass, in order to maintain the tightness and unity of the section.

TRACK 33 — Full Band
TRACK 34 — Slow Demo

Guitar Solo

Hetfield accompanies the first eight bars of the guitar solo with a one-bar riff. The ninth and tenth bars contain unison triplets, which were first heard before the solo and derive from the sixteenth-note triplets in the interlude. Newsted plays the triplets in octaves. During the remainder of the solo Newsted, mimicking Hetfield and Ulrich, primarily plays a rhythm comprised of two beats of eighth-note triplets followed by two quarter notes. Pitches are adjusted to suit the harmony of each bar.

Full Band

Enter Sandman

from *Metallica*

Words and Music by
James Hetfield, Lars Ulrich and Kirk Hammett

"Enter Sandman," with its radio-friendly song structure, slick production, and heavy-rotation on MTV, marked Metallica's transformation from cult heroes into pop icons.

Introduction

"Enter Sandman" has the form of a typical pop song—intro, verse, chorus, verse, solo, middle-eight, chorus, end—something Metallica had not done on any previous album. It starts with the main riff played on acoustic guitar over Ulrich's hi-hat quarter notes. When Ulrich switches to a rock beat, Hetfield continues playing the opening riff for 16 more bars, but he now does so on a distorted electric guitar in a reductionist, somewhat minimalist manner. The bass enters halfway through and keeps a steady heartbeat pulse with the drums. The phrases become more and more layered with each repetion, as more instruments enter, leading up to the tritone-tainted E pedal in Bass Fig. 2 (bar 29). Check out how Newsted's use of ties give the music a sense of forward motion.

TRACK 36

Full Band

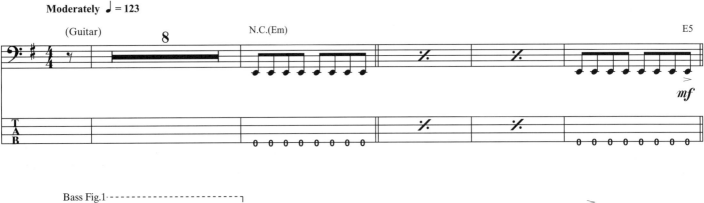

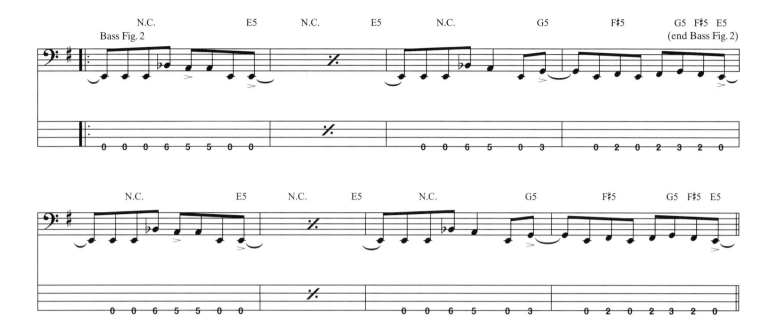

Pre-Chorus and Chorus

The four-bar pre-chorus is played with a half time feel with the bass and drums accenting beats 1, the "and" of 1, and 3. The chorus is a seven-bar passage: a four-bar riff, a repetition of the riff's latter two bars, and a seventh, contrasting bar. This section presents a simple rock and roll groove, with a straightforward $\frac{4}{4}$ drum beat and a steady, eighth-note pulse in the bass. Again, notice how Newsted's use of ties, across the bar line, help to add drama to the music. A bass and drum break concludes the section.

TRACK 37

Full Band

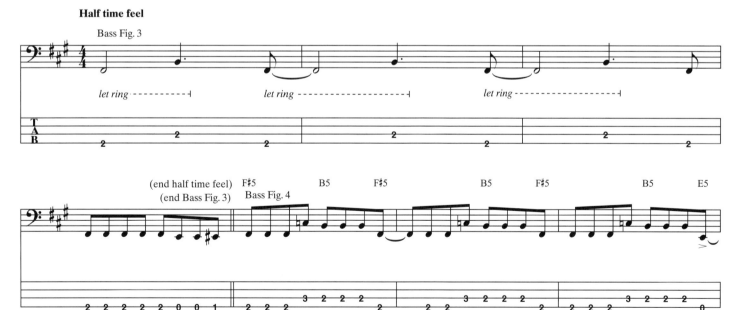

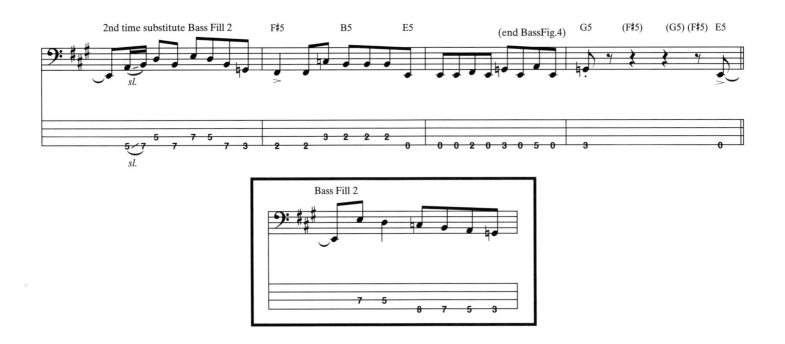

Guitar Solo

The form of the guitar solo is exactly the same as one pass through the verse/pre-chorus/chorus section, so Newsted plays accordingly. The last four bars of the solo are interesting in that they return to Bass Fig.1 (from the introduction), this time with only a lead guitar on top. This creative use of earlier material provides a smooth lead-in to the next section, which features the voices of Hetfield and the child in responsive prayer.

TRACK 38

Full Band

Half time feel

(end half time feel)

Sad but True

from *Metallica*

Words and Music by
James Hetfield and Lars Ulrich

The restraint heard throughout *Metallica* represented a shift away from the musical complexity that increased from album to album and culminated in their technical tour de force ... *And Justice For All.* This new, simpler aesthetic is nowhere more apparent than in "Sad but True"

Introduction

The first four-bar riff is a slow, steady dirge alternating between two chords that are a half step apart. The bass part supports this harmonic move—which returns in the interlude section just before the guitar solo—and even embellishes it a little in bar 6 with a small fill. At the end of the riff's second pass, the whole group stops on beat 1 with a short attack and rests for the remainder of the bar.

The second intro riff, while technically a four-bar riff, is really a one-bar idea with a different ending the fourth time it is played. The riff is heavy and bluesy, and Newsted doubles it in order to thicken the texture and strengthen the groove. Make sure that the pull-offs are accurate, yet sound relaxed and are in-sync with the guitars. After the second pass of the riff, there are two extra bars in which its ending is repeated.

TRACK 39

Full Band

TRACK 40

Slow Demo

Moderately slow ♩ = 86

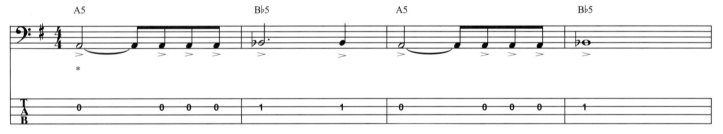

*Tune down 3½ steps (④ = A, ③ = D, ②= G, ① = C); tuning simulates the bottom 4 strings of a 5-stg. bass, tuned down one whole step.

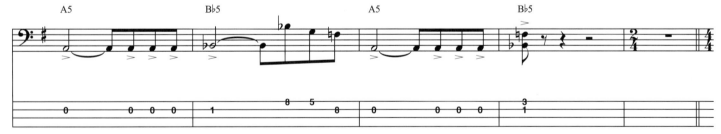

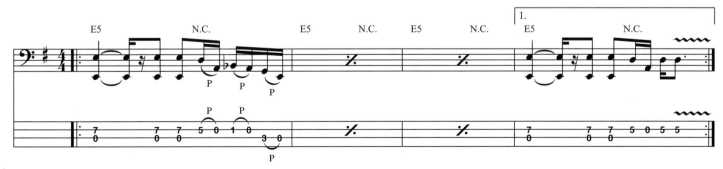

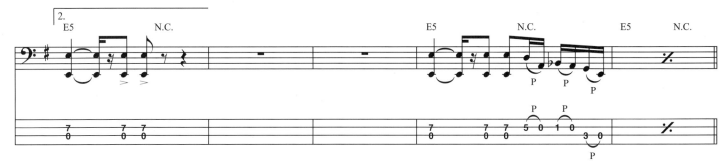

Verse

Newsted's two-bar phrase here corresponds with the two-bar guitar riff that drives the verse. The built-in pauses in the bass pattern contrast with the balls-out rock groove of the drums, and together they form a tight rhythmic background for the vocals. Notice the signature tritone leaps from E to B♭.

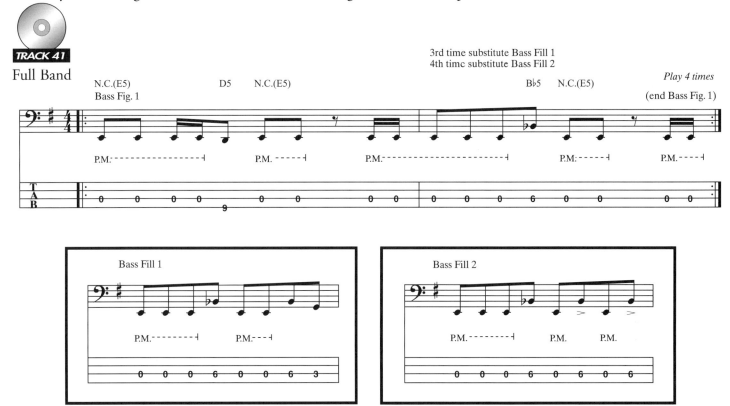

Chorus

The rhythmic motive ♪♩♪♩, first heard in the bass part of the verse, is expanded on in the chorus. Initially the figure was used to keep an E pedal active. This figure is now used to gradually propel the melodic movement of the bass upwards, culminating in the C ensemble triplet hit on beat 2 of bar 4. Also check out the A♭ passing tone in bar 3 and note its careful, unobtrusive placement—subtle and slick.

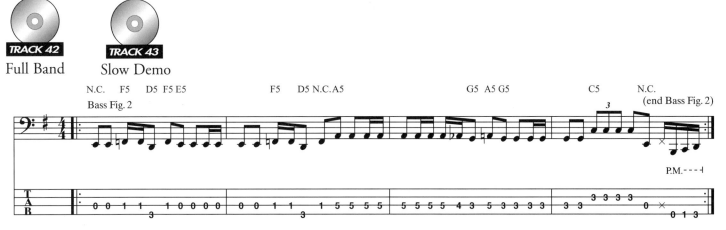

Guitar Solo

The guitar solo is first played over six repetitions of the first bar of the second intro riff. Starting in bar 7, Metallica plays four repetitions of a new, one-bar riff whose chord progression is motivically related to the opening half step move. The rhythm of this bass part is tricky; before you try to play it, tap the rhythm while counting the beats out loud.

TRACK 44

Full Band

The Unforgiven

from *Metallica*

Words and Music by
James Hetfield, Lars Ulrich and Kirk Hammett

Orchestration in a Metallica song? With the opening crescendo of trumpet and snare followed by alternating chime and castanet figures, this sounds like a scene from a western. Hearing it, you can picture a cowboy strolling through town, or maybe a shootout down at the creek. It is an appropriate musical style, considering the lyrics of the song.

Introduction and Verse

After a rich texture of classical guitar, electric guitar, castanets, and snare drum is established, the bass and drums enter in bar 9. For the next four bars, Newsted's bass part doubles the prominent notes of the electric guitar melody, while leaving just enough space for the guitar to add embellishments. The introduction then concludes with two more bars of the A-minor tonic chord.

Even though it is slow and simple, Newsted's groove in the verse is deceptively tricky to play precisely, especially coming from the double time feel arpeggiated guitar accompaniment in the intro. When the tempo is this slow, the tendency is to rush. If you find this to be a problem as you play this part, isolate a two-bar fragment, and using a metronome at a slow tempo (such as ♩=69, the tempo of this song), play these two bars over and over, creating a loop. As you repeat these two bars, listen carefully to make sure your downbeats are always lining up with the metronome clicks and that eighth and sixteenth note figures are evenly spaced between the clicks.

TRACK 45

Full Band

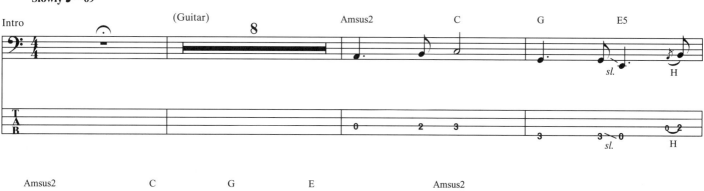

The Unforgiven *Cont.*

Guitar Solo

Though it is played in a grungier, more intense way, the music under the guitar solo is identical to that described in the verse—the only difference is the $\frac{4}{4}$ bar at the end, which functions as a link back to the cho-rus. Newsted plays mostly the same material, but with more fills and greater energy. Practice the continual sixteenth-note fills with a metronome until you can play them evenly and without loosening the groove.

Nothing Else Matters

from *Metallica*

Words and Music by
James Hetfield and Lars Ulrich

The ballad "Nothing Else Matters" has all of the trademark Metallica arranging elements—acoustic guitar intro, twin-harmony leads, and a triumphant guitar solo—but this time in a more subdued, contemporary package that has none of the obligatory accompanying scorch associated with the typical metal ballad. This stylistic malleability enables Metallica to remain at the forefront of current musical trends while still maintaining their voice.

Clean Guitar Solo

The backdrop for this clean guitar solo is two passes of a simple harmonic progression, Em–Am–C–D–Em. This progression has an interesting, "deceptive," harmonic feature built in: C–D tend to function as IV–V of G major, but here they lead instead to its relative minor, E minor. This technique, known as a *deceptive cadence,* is used to prolong a section, and it is this wandering, somewhat unresolved quality that makes it so appropriate for this wistful solo. The ♫ figure that occurs on beats 3 and 6, just before the strong beats of the § meter, in Newsted's bass part, adds subtle movement to the texture without stealing any attention from the solo.

TRACK 48

Full Band

TRACK 49

Slow Demo

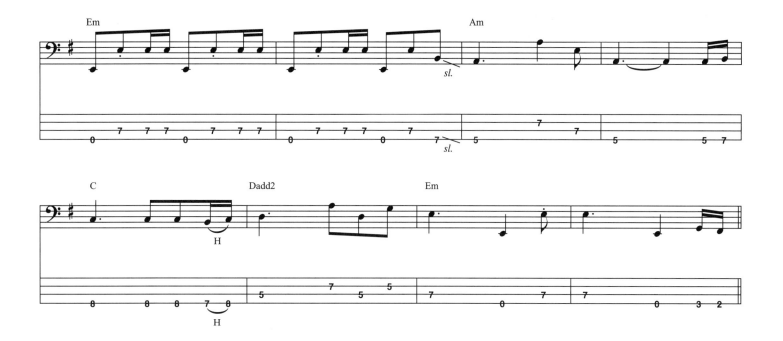

Distorted Guitar Solo

As a member of an ensemble, it is always important to be aware of how your role relates to the big picture—to "think global," as environmentalists often say. For example, because the solo is played with a distorted guitar sound rather than clean, Newsted took the liberty of playing more heavily in this section. In your own musical interactions with other players, always try to hear how your part fits into the overall sound, just as Newsted did here.

TRACK 50

Full Band

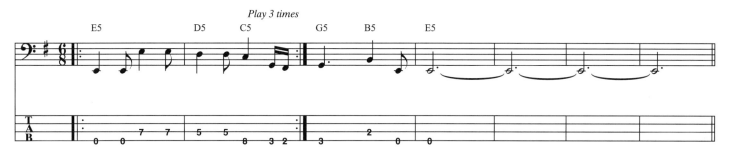

Until It Sleeps

from *Load*

Words and Music by
James Hetfield and Lars Ulrich

The sound here is reminiscent of instrumental surf music. Hetfield appropriately strives to infuse his singing with more tone and less growl. Newsted also uses a new sound here—fretless bass. It is not necessary for you to play the song on a fretless, however, you should try to match Newsted's tone as closely as possible.

Introduction/Verse/Chorus

The rhythm of this intro and verse is complicated by the irregular relationship between the syncopation of the bass line and the sextuplet rolls that Ulrich plays on the last beat of his two-bar pattern. Listening closely may even create the illusion that the drums are out of sync! To prevent any confusion, practice with a metronome and learn the part until you can play it in your sleep (no pun intended). Play along with the drums only when you feel comfortable with the line on its own. Also, be on guard not to rush this section, as the drum fills may give you that inclination.

In the eight-bar chorus section, Newsted plays steady eighth notes that are interrupted by syncopated quarter notes. A four-bar interlude follows the chorus and sets up the next verse. It consists of two passes through the guitar riff that was heard in the verse, the second of which is slightly altered in order to flow more smoothly into the verse.

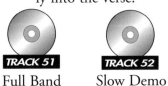

TRACK 51   TRACK 52
Full Band   Slow Demo

Moderate Rock ♩ = 120

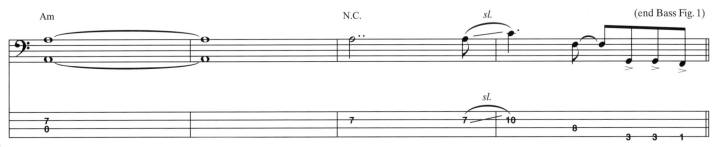

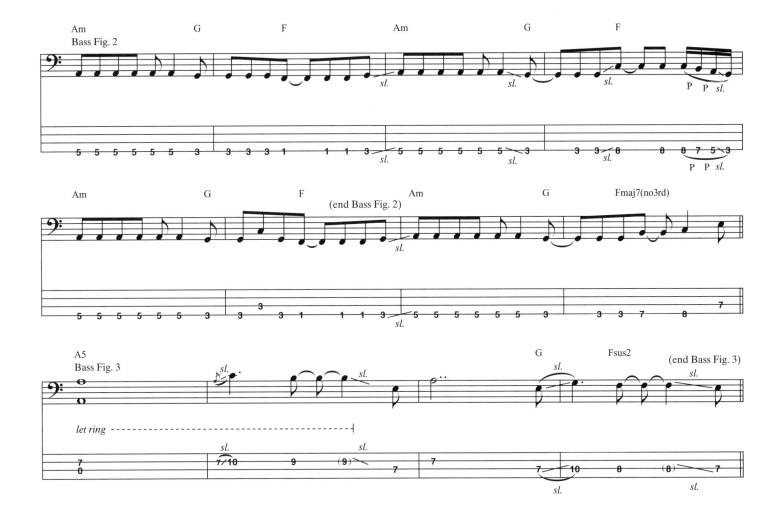

Bridge

This section moves in a smooth-sounding $\frac{6}{4}$ groove. Newsted's part nicely complements the guitar parts with octaves and double-stops, using the open E string as an anchor to thicken the texture and highlight the melodic movement of the guitar part (D–D♯–E).

TRACK 53
Full Band

TRACK 54
Slow Demo

King Nothing

from *Load*

Words and Music by
James Hetfield, Lars Ulrich and Kirk Hammett

The lyrics of "King Nothing" offer an interesting look into the insipid desires of the greedy and vacuous. The quirky opening bass riff in conjunction with the buzzing guitar noise complement this social commentary on the absurd perfectly.

Introduction

The introduction to "King Nothing" is an example of good ensemble arranging. Newsted enters with a funky, ultra-chromatic bass line midway through a long fade-in that consists of a hi-hat and a buzzing guitar feedback effect. As Newsted enters, the guitar continues to buzz and the hi-hat continues ticking. At the fifth repetition of the bass riff, the guitar finally joins in, breaking away from its role as a textural device and doubling the bass riff. The staggering of instrument entrances in this arrangement adds excitement and heightens the sense of anticipation, while sounding organic and uncontrived.

TRACK 55

Full Band

Bridge

In a move that is common but always effective, Metallica switches here to a half time feel. Newsted plays mostly A's in two different octaves, but in the second and fourth bars, Newsted also plays an accented E♭ on the "and" of 2. Since the root harmony of the passage is A, E♭ is a tritone away; this is similar to the prominent B♭'s in the introduction, which formed a tritone with the root E.

TRACK 56

Full Band

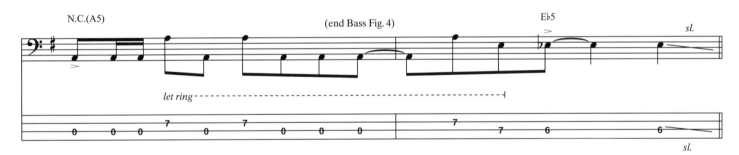

Fuel

from *Reload*

Words and Music by
James Hetfield, Lars Ulrich and Kirk Hammett

In keeping with the subject of the lyrics, this song really burns with high energy! Tightness is the key to pulling it off, so pay attention to the constant tempo changes and the nuances of Newsted's intense playing.

Introduction

Hetfield sings in the first two bars and then plays half of the first intro riff. Two bars after the entrance of the guitar, the first intro riff is stated in its full, four-bar length (it is actually a one-bar pattern repeated three times and altered the fourth). The accents in Newsted's bass part divide the bar's eight eighth notes into 3+3+2. After two passes through the riff, Metallica switches to a half time feel and then goes straight into the second riff, which is also a one-bar pattern altered every fourth pass. After just one pass through the second riff, there is a switch back to a normal-time feel with the two bars of the first riff, which sets up the verse.

TRACK 57
Full Band

TRACK 58
Slow Demo

59

Verses 1 and 2

During the verse riff, Ulrich returns to a half time feel, but plays quarter notes on the hi-hat—this continuous alternation between half time and regular feels is one of the most fun aspects of the song. Newsted's bass line follows suit and he uses some hip, rhythmic devices to generate interest. His accenting of beat 4 in bar 3 creates the illusion that the downbeat has been shifted and gives life to what could have been another typical blues scale line. Also, notice how in bars 6–7 and 20–21, Newsted takes an idea and transposes it to accomodate the chord change (B5–B♭5). After the second pass of the verse riff, the second intro riff returns, followed once again by two bars of the first intro riff. Newsted's accompaniments are similar to those he played when these ideas occurred in the introduction. The second verse is very similar musically to the first, except that there are four bars of the first intro riff, now with an added chromatic run at the end, instead of just two.

TRACK 59

Full Band

Chorus and Tag

The driving, eighth-note bass line and double bass drum part establish a tight rhythmic groove. Notice how Newsted's subtle use of connecting passing tones (G$\sharp$ in bars 2, 6, 10, and A$\sharp$ in bar 12) make the chord changes smooth and seamless—keep this idea in mind when creating your own bass lines. To achieve maximum precision, use a pick when playing this section.

TRACK 60

Full Band

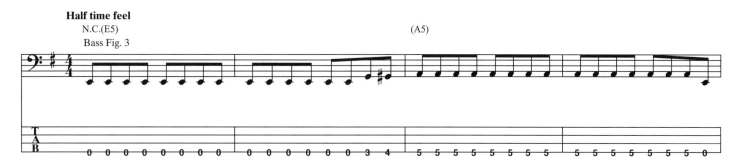

Fuel Cont.

The Memory Remains

from *Reload*

Words and Music by
James Hetfield and Lars Ulrich

"The Memory Remains" pays homage to the riff masters of the early 1970s by way of its plodding rhythms and structural simplicity.

Introduction

After Hetfield sings a phrase from the chorus accompanied only by guitar, the group starts the intro/verse riff. This slow, Black Sabbath-esque groove is essentially three repetitions of a two-bar pattern followed by three tag bars (for an unusual total of nine!). Although it looks easy on the page, it takes a lot of concentration to make such a slow groove feel right. In order to establish the fluid feeling that is needed, hesitate when playing the first beat of each bar. (To understand this technique, you may want to listen to the song "Iron Man" on Black Sabbath's *Paranoid,* which is where it was invented.) This is one of only a few Metallica songs that never deviates from a slow, half time feel.

TRACK 61

Full Band

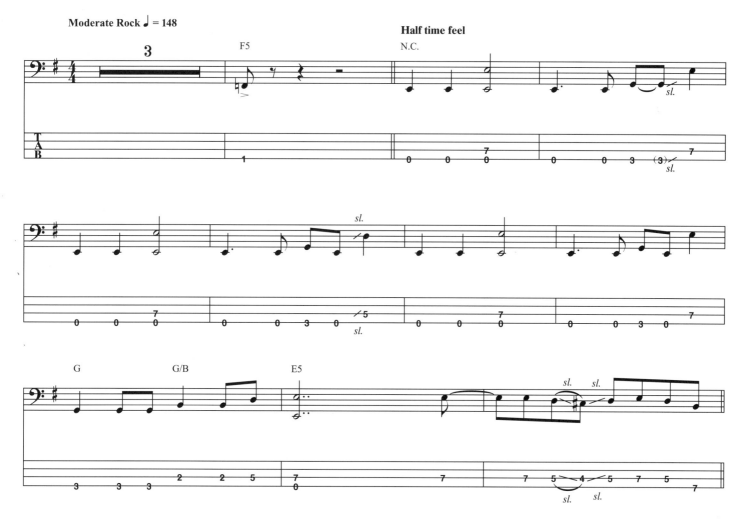

Guitar Solo

This nine-bar solo begins with a pickup bar of eighth notes played by the guitar alone. It is played over the same material as was the intro riff. You have probably noticed by now that Newsted (like all good musicians who understand the chemistry of an ensemble) tends to plays simple parts during solos so as not to divert the spotlight from where it belongs; this solo is no exception and should serve as an example of the art of accompanying.

TRACK 62
Full Band